Options Trading for Beginners: Unlocking the Power of Derivatives

Copyright (c) 2024 by Adam Holzer

All rights reserved. No part of this book may be reproduced in any form or by any electronic or mechanical means, including information storage and retrieval systems, without permission in writing from the publisher, except by a reviewer who may quote brief passages in a review.

Chapter 1: Understanding the Basics of Options

Chapter 2: Key Concepts in Options Trading

Chapter 3: The Mechanics of Options Trading

Chapter 4: Strategies for Beginners

Chapter 5: Pricing and Valuation of Options

Chapter 6: Risk Management in Options Trading

Chapter 7: Advanced Concepts (Optional for Ambitious Beginners)

Chapter 8: Tools and Resources for Options Traders

Chapter 9: Building Your Options Trading Plan

Chapter 10: The Path Forward: From Beginner to Pro

Conclusion

Introduction

If you've ever wondered how professional traders make money beyond buying and selling stocks, or if you're simply curious about what options trading is and how it works, this book is the perfect place to start.

Options trading might sound complicated at first, with its unique terminology and strategies, but the truth is that anyone can learn to trade options with the right guidance. Whether you're looking to diversify your investments, protect your portfolio, or generate additional income, understanding options can open up a world of possibilities in the financial markets.

This book is designed for absolute beginners—no prior experience or advanced math skills are required. It's written with one goal in mind: to make options trading simple, relatable, and actionable. Throughout these chapters, we'll break down complex concepts into manageable steps, using real-world examples to ensure everything makes sense.

By the time you finish this book, you'll not only know what options are but also understand how to use them effectively. You'll learn about the key strategies, risks, and tools involved in options trading. More importantly, you'll gain the confidence to take your first steps into the world of derivatives.

If you're ready to unlock the power of options and take control of your financial future, let's dive in!

Chapter 1: Understanding the Basics of Options

Options trading is a fascinating way to participate in financial markets. Whether you're looking to enhance your investment portfolio or explore new trading strategies, understanding the basics of options is a crucial first step. This chapter introduces you to the world of derivatives, the role of options in the financial markets, the different types of options, and how they compare to traditional stock trading.

What Are Derivatives?

Definition of Derivatives

At their core, derivatives are financial contracts that derive their value from an underlying asset. These assets can range from stocks and commodities to indices, currencies, or even interest rates.

For example, if you own a derivative tied to the price of gold, the value of that derivative will fluctuate based on changes in the price of gold.

The Role of Options in the Derivatives Market

Options are one of the most commonly traded derivatives. They offer traders and investors flexibility by allowing them to speculate on price movements, hedge against risk, or generate income—all without requiring them to own the underlying asset.

The derivatives market serves a vital role in the financial system by:

- Providing liquidity to markets
- Helping businesses and investors manage financial risk
- Offering tools for speculation and investment

Types of Options

Options come in two main types, each serving a unique purpose in the financial markets:

1. Call Options

A call option gives the holder the right, but not the obligation, to buy an underlying asset at a specific price (known as the strike price) within a set time frame.

- **When to Use:** Traders buy call options when they expect the price of the underlying asset to rise.

- **Example:** If you purchase a call option for a stock with a strike price of $100, and the stock rises to $120, you can buy the stock at $100 and potentially sell it for $120, locking in a profit.

2. Put Options

A put option gives the holder the right, but not the obligation, to sell an underlying asset at a specific strike price within a set time frame.

- **When to Use:** Traders buy put options when they expect the price of the underlying asset to fall.

- **Example:** If you purchase a put option for a stock with a strike price of $80, and the stock drops to $60, you can sell the stock at $80, securing a profit.

Options vs. Stocks

Although options and stocks are both integral parts of the financial markets, they differ significantly in how they work and the opportunities they offer:

Key Differences

- **Ownership:** Stocks represent ownership in a company, while options are contracts that give the holder rights to buy or sell an asset.

- **Capital Requirement:** Options allow you to control more of the underlying asset with less capital compared to buying stocks outright.

- **Expiration:** Options have an expiration date, while stocks can be held indefinitely.

Pros and Cons of Trading Options vs. Stocks

- **Pros of Options:**
  - Lower initial investment compared to stocks

- Flexibility to profit in various market conditions (up, down, or sideways)

- Tools for hedging and risk management

- **Cons of Options:**

- Options are time-sensitive and can expire worthless

- More complex compared to buying and holding stocks

- Higher risk if not managed properly

Trading stocks may feel more straightforward for beginners, but options provide unparalleled versatility once you understand their mechanics.

Notes:

- Derivatives, including options, derive their value from an underlying asset and play a vital role in financial markets.

- Call options give you the right to buy an asset, while put options give you the right to sell it.

- Options differ from stocks in terms of ownership, capital requirements, and risk profiles, offering unique advantages for traders and investors.

Chapter 2: Key Concepts in Options Trading

Understanding options trading starts with mastering its core concepts and terminology. In this chapter, we'll break down the key language of options, explain how options work, and introduce you to the participants in the market. By the end, you'll have a solid foundation to build your options trading knowledge.

The Language of Options

Options trading comes with a unique set of terms that are essential to grasp:

Strike Price

The strike price is the predetermined price at which the buyer of an option can buy (for a call) or sell (for a put) the underlying asset. It's the cornerstone of an options contract and determines its profitability.

- **Example:** If you buy a call option with a strike price

of $50, you can purchase the stock at $50 regardless of its current market price.

Expiry Date

Options contracts don't last forever—they have an expiry date. This is the date by which the holder must decide to exercise the option or let it expire.

- Short-term options (weekly or monthly) have a closer expiry, while long-term options (LEAPs) can last for years.

Premiums

The premium is the price you pay to purchase an options contract. It's determined by factors like the underlying asset's price, time to expiration, and market volatility.

- **Example:** If a call option has a premium of $5 and you buy one contract (representing 100 shares), the total cost is $500.

How Options Work

Options are versatile tools, but understanding how they function is crucial:

Exercising Options

Exercising an option means you choose to use your right to buy (call) or sell (put) the underlying asset at the strike price. However, many options traders don't exercise their contracts—instead, they sell them in the market before expiration to capture profits.

In-the-Money (ITM), At-the-Money (ATM), and Out-of-the-Money (OTM)

Options contracts can be categorized based on their relationship to the strike price:

- **In-the-Money (ITM):** The option has intrinsic value. For calls, this means the stock price is above the strike price. For puts, it's below.

- **At-the-Money (ATM):** The stock price is equal to the strike price.

- **Out-of-the-Money (OTM):** The option has no intrinsic value. For calls, the stock price is below the strike price. For puts, it's above.

- **Example:** If a stock is trading at $100:
- A call option with a $90 strike price is in-the-money.
- A call option with a $100 strike price is at-the-money.
- A call option with a $110 strike price is out-of-the-money.

Participants in the Market

The options market is made up of various participants, each with different objectives:

Buyers vs. Sellers

- **Buyers:** Pay the premium for the right to buy or sell the underlying asset. Their potential losses are limited to the premium paid, but their potential gains can be significant.

- **Sellers (Writers):** Receive the premium but take on the obligation to buy or sell the asset if the buyer exercises the option. Sellers face higher risks, as their potential losses can be substantial.

Speculators, Hedgers, and Arbitrageurs

- **Speculators:** Trade options to profit from price movements in the underlying asset. They aim to buy low and sell high (or vice versa).

- **Hedgers:** Use options to protect their portfolios from adverse price changes. For example, an investor might buy put options as insurance against a stock's decline.

- **Arbitrageurs:** Seek risk-free profits by exploiting price discrepancies between the options market and the underlying asset. Their trades help keep markets efficient.

Notes:

- Mastering the language of options—strike price, expiry date, and premiums—is essential to understanding how they work.

- Options can be in-the-money, at-the-money, or out-of-the-money depending on their relationship to the strike price.

- The market is driven by participants with different goals: speculators aim for profit, hedgers seek protection, and arbitrageurs ensure market efficiency.

Chapter 3: The Mechanics of Options Trading

Now that you understand the basics of options, it's time to dive into the practical side of trading. This chapter will walk you through the steps of setting up an account, understanding the key data points in an options chain, and executing your first trade.

How to Start Trading Options

Setting Up a Brokerage Account

To trade options, you'll need to open an account with a brokerage that offers options trading. Here's how to get started:

1. **Research Brokers:** Look for brokers with low fees, robust trading platforms, and educational resources for beginners.

2. **Application Process:** Most brokers require you to complete an options trading application. You'll answer

questions about your investment experience, financial background, and trading goals.

3. **Approval Levels:** Brokers assign trading approval levels based on your experience. Beginners typically start with basic strategies like buying calls and puts.

Understanding Margin Requirements

Some options trades require a margin account, which lets you borrow money or leverage your assets to execute trades. Margin can amplify gains but also increases risk.

- For beginners, focus on strategies that don't require margin (e.g., buying calls and puts) until you gain more experience.

Reading an Options Chain

An options chain is a table that displays available options contracts for a specific underlying asset. Learning to interpret this data is crucial for making informed trades.

Key Data Points in an Options Chain

1. **Strike Price:** The price at which the option can be exercised.

2. **Expiry Date:** The date when the option contract expires.

3. **Premium:** The cost of the option, which consists of intrinsic value and time value.

4. **Bid and Ask Prices:** The highest price a buyer is willing to pay (bid) and the lowest price a seller is willing to accept (ask).

5. **Open Interest:** The total number of outstanding contracts for a particular strike price and expiry date.

6. **Implied Volatility (IV):** A measure of the market's expectations for future price fluctuations of the underlying asset.

How to Choose a Contract

Selecting the right options contract depends on your trading strategy, market outlook, and risk tolerance:

1. **Define Your Objective:** Are you speculating on price movements, hedging risk, or generating income?

2. **Pick a Strike Price:** Choose a strike price that aligns with your expectations for the underlying asset's price movement.

- In-the-money options have higher premiums but greater chances of profitability.

- Out-of-the-money options are cheaper but require significant price movement to be profitable.

3. **Select an Expiry Date:** Short-term contracts are more volatile but less expensive, while long-term contracts (LEAPs) provide more stability.

Executing a Trade

Placing Orders

Once you've chosen your options contract, it's time to place an order. There are several order types to understand:

- **Market Order:** Buys or sells the option at the current market price.

- **Limit Order:** Sets a specific price at which you're willing to buy or sell the option.

- **Stop Order:** Executes the trade once the option reaches a specified price, limiting potential losses.

Understanding Settlement

Options trades settle differently than stock trades:

- **T+1 Settlement:** Most options trades settle one business day after the trade date (compared to T+2 for stocks).

- **Exercise and Assignment:** If an option is exercised, the underlying asset is transferred between the buyer and seller. If you're assigned on a short position, you're obligated to fulfill the contract terms.

Notes:

- Setting up a brokerage account and understanding margin requirements are the first steps to trading options.

- The options chain provides critical data points like strike prices, premiums, and implied volatility to help you make informed decisions.

- Choosing the right contract involves balancing your objectives, risk tolerance, and market outlook.

- Placing orders and understanding settlement processes are essential for executing trades confidently.

Chapter 4: Strategies for Beginners

Trading options can seem intimidating at first, but starting with beginner-friendly strategies helps you build confidence and minimize risk. This chapter introduces straightforward, single-leg strategies, income-generating methods, and key pitfalls to avoid. By focusing on simplicity and discipline, you can set yourself up for a successful options trading journey.

Single-Leg Strategies

Single-leg strategies involve trading one options contract at a time. These are the simplest and most accessible strategies for beginners.

1. Buying Calls

Buying a call option gives you the right (but not the obligation) to buy the underlying asset at a specific strike price before the expiry date.

- **Objective:** You profit when the price of the

underlying asset rises above the strike price, plus the premium you paid.

- **Example:**

- You buy a call option for Stock XYZ with a strike price of $50 and a premium of $2.

- If XYZ rises to $60, the option's intrinsic value is $10, netting you $8 per share after deducting the premium.

- **When to Use:** When you're bullish on the underlying asset and expect significant price appreciation.

- **Advantages:**

- Low initial investment compared to buying stocks.

- Potential for high returns if the asset rises significantly.

- **Risks:**

- The option can expire worthless if the price stays below the strike price.

- Entire premium paid is at risk.

2. Buying Puts

Buying a put option gives you the right to sell the underlying asset at a specific strike price before the expiry date.

- **Objective:** You profit when the price of the underlying asset falls below the strike price, minus the premium you paid.

- **Example:**

- You buy a put option for Stock ABC with a strike price of $80 and a premium of $3.

- If ABC falls to $70, the option's intrinsic value is $10, netting you $7 per share after deducting the premium.

- When to Use: When you're bearish on the underlying asset and expect its price to decline.

- **Advantages:**

- Low-cost way to profit from falling markets.

- Acts as insurance if you already own the stock.

- **Risks:**

- The option can expire worthless if the price stays above the strike price.

- The premium paid is your maximum loss.

Income-Generating Strategies

For beginners seeking consistent returns, income-generating strategies like covered calls and cash-secured puts are great options.

1. Covered Calls

A covered call involves owning a stock and selling a call option on that stock.

- **Objective:** Generate income from the premium while potentially selling the stock at a favorable price if the option is exercised.

- **Example:**

- You own 100 shares of Stock DEF, currently trading at $50 per share.

- You sell a call option with a strike price of $55 and receive a premium of $2 per share.

- If DEF stays below $55, the option expires, and you keep the premium.

- If DEF rises above $55, the option is exercised, and

you sell your shares for $55, plus the $2 premium.

- **When to Use:** When you're neutral or slightly bullish on the stock and want to generate additional income.

- **Advantages:**

- Earn extra income from stocks you already own.

- Offers some downside protection.

- **Risks:**

- Limited upside potential if the stock price surges.

- You may be forced to sell your shares if the option is exercised.

2. Cash-Secured Puts

A cash-secured put involves selling a put option while holding enough cash to buy the stock if the option is exercised.

- **Objective:** Earn premium income while potentially buying the stock at a discount if the price falls below the strike price.

- **Example:**

- You sell a put option on Stock GHI with a strike price

of $40 and receive a $3 premium.

- If GHI falls below $40, you're obligated to buy 100 shares at $40, effectively paying $37 per share after factoring in the premium.

- If GHI stays above $40, the option expires, and you keep the premium.

- When to Use: When you're bullish on a stock and willing to own it at a lower price.

- **Advantages:**

- Generate income while waiting for the stock to reach your target price.

- Reduces the effective purchase price of the stock.

- **Risks:**

- You may end up buying the stock if it falls significantly, locking in a potential unrealized loss.

Common Mistakes to Avoid

Beginning traders often fall into avoidable traps. Here are two of the most common pitfalls:

1. Overleveraging

Options trading can be tempting because of the high potential for returns. However, overleveraging—investing too much of your capital in options—can quickly lead to significant losses.

- **Why It Happens:** Beginners underestimate the risk of options expiring worthless.

- **How to Avoid:**

- Start small and allocate only a portion of your portfolio to options.

- Avoid using margin until you fully understand the risks.

2. Misjudging Market Trends

Accurately predicting market direction is challenging, even for experienced traders. Misjudging trends can lead to poor trade decisions.

- **Why It Happens:** Beginners often rely on emotions or incomplete analysis.

- **How to Avoid:**

- Conduct thorough research and use technical and fundamental analysis to inform your trades.

- Be disciplined about using stop-loss orders to minimize losses.

Notes:

- Single-leg strategies, such as buying calls and puts, are ideal starting points for beginners, offering straightforward ways to profit from market movements.

- Income-generating strategies like covered calls and cash-secured puts provide consistent returns and are excellent for risk-averse traders.

- Avoid common pitfalls by managing your risk, starting small, and ensuring your trades are based on solid research, not speculation or overconfidence.

Chapter 5: Pricing and Valuation of Options

Understanding the factors that influence an option's price is critical for making informed trading decisions. Options pricing is more complex than simply observing the market value of the underlying asset—it incorporates various components that reflect the contract's potential profitability, risk, and time sensitivity. This chapter delves into the key aspects of options pricing, including intrinsic and time value, the Greeks, and the role of volatility.

The Components of an Option's Price

An option's price, also known as its **premium**, consists of two main components: intrinsic value and time value.

1. Intrinsic Value

Intrinsic value represents the real, tangible value of the option if it were exercised immediately.

- **For Call Options:**

  - Intrinsic value = Current price of the underlying asset − Strike price.

  - Example: If a call option's strike price is $50 and the underlying asset is trading at $60, the intrinsic value is $10.

- **For Put Options:**

  - Intrinsic value = Strike price − Current price of the underlying asset.

  - Example: If a put option's strike price is $50 and the underlying asset is trading at $40, the intrinsic value is $10.

- **Key Point:** Options that are **in-the-money (ITM)** have intrinsic value, while those that are **at-the-money (ATM)** or **out-of-the-money (OTM)** do not.

2. Time Value

Time value reflects the additional premium an investor is willing to pay for the potential that the option will become profitable before expiration.

- **Formula:** Time value = Option premium − Intrinsic value.

- **Factors Influencing Time Value:**

- **Time to Expiry:** The longer the time until expiration, the higher the time value.

- **Volatility:** More volatile underlying assets have higher time value due to the increased likelihood of significant price movement.

- **Interest Rates:** Changes in interest rates can also impact time value.

The Greeks: Measuring Risk

The **Greeks** are metrics used to quantify the risks and sensitivities of an option's price to various factors. These metrics help traders understand how changes in the market will impact their options.

1. Delta: Price Sensitivity

Delta measures how much the price of an option will change for every $1 move in the underlying asset's price.

- **For Call Options:** Delta ranges from 0 to 1. A delta of

0.5 means the option price will increase by $0.50 for every $1 increase in the underlying asset.

- **For Put Options:** Delta ranges from -1 to 0. A delta of -0.5 means the option price will decrease by $0.50 for every $1 increase in the underlying asset.

- **Key Insight:** Delta also represents the probability that an option will expire in-the-money.

2. Gamma: Rate of Change

Gamma measures the rate of change of delta as the underlying asset's price moves.

- High gamma indicates that delta will change significantly for small price movements, making the option more sensitive.

- Gamma is highest for ATM options and decreases as options move ITM or OTM.

3. Theta: Time Decay

Theta represents the rate at which an option's price declines as it approaches expiration, assuming all other factors remain constant.

- **Key Insight:** Time decay accelerates as expiration nears, particularly for short-term options.

- **Impact on Traders:** Buyers of options lose value over time due to theta, while sellers (writers) benefit from time decay.

4. Vega: Volatility Impact

Vega measures the sensitivity of an option's price to changes in implied volatility.

- High vega means the option's price is more influenced by volatility.

- **Key Insight:** Options with longer time to expiration have higher vega, as increased volatility has a greater impact on their potential profitability.

Volatility's Role in Pricing

Volatility plays a crucial role in determining an option's premium, as it affects the likelihood of significant price movement in the underlying asset.

1. Implied Volatility (IV)

Implied volatility reflects the market's expectations for future price fluctuations of the underlying asset.

- **High IV:** Indicates that the market anticipates significant price swings, leading to higher premiums.

- **Low IV:** Suggests that the market expects less volatility, resulting in lower premiums.

- **Key Insight:** IV tends to increase during periods of market uncertainty and decrease during periods of stability.

2. Historical Volatility (HV)

Historical volatility measures the actual price fluctuations of the underlying asset over a specific period in the past.

- **Comparison with IV:** Traders often compare IV and HV to identify opportunities:

- **When IV > HV:** Options may be overpriced, presenting a selling opportunity.

- **When IV < HV:** Options may be underpriced,

presenting a buying opportunity.

Practical Examples of Pricing and Valuation

Example 1: Call Option Pricing

- Underlying asset price: $100
- Strike price: $95
- Premium: $8
- Intrinsic value = $100 - $95 = $5
- Time value = $8 - $5 = $3

Example 2: Impact of Volatility on Premiums

- A call option with a strike price of $50 has a premium of $5 at 20% IV.
- If IV rises to 30%, the premium increases to $8 due to the higher likelihood of significant price movement.

Notes:

- An option's price consists of intrinsic value (based on the underlying asset's price) and time value (reflecting potential future profitability).

- The Greeks—delta, gamma, theta, and vega—provide valuable insights into how options prices react to changes in market conditions.

- Volatility, both implied and historical, significantly influences an option's premium and can present trading opportunities.

- Understanding these pricing and valuation components is essential for making informed trading decisions and managing risk effectively.

Chapter 6: Risk Management in Options Trading

Risk management is a cornerstone of successful options trading. While options offer the potential for substantial profits, they also carry significant risks. This chapter will guide you through identifying and managing risk, implementing effective strategies to protect your capital, and maintaining a disciplined mindset to navigate the psychological challenges of trading.

Identifying and Managing Risk

Risk in options trading can stem from several factors, including market volatility, time decay, and misjudged strategies. Proper risk management begins with identifying these risks and creating a plan to mitigate them.

1. The Importance of Risk Assessment

- **Understand the Risk/Reward Ratio:** Every trade should have a clearly defined risk/reward ratio. For example, risking $1 to potentially make $3 represents a favorable ratio.

- **Assess Market Conditions:** Analyze trends, volatility, and economic indicators to anticipate potential price movements.

- **Evaluate Worst-Case Scenarios:** Consider what happens if the trade moves against you and ensure you can handle the potential loss.

Setting Stop-Loss and Profit Targets

Establishing predefined exit points for each trade can help protect your capital and lock in profits.

1. Stop-Loss Orders

- Set a price level at which you will exit the trade to minimize losses.

- Example: If you buy a call option at $5, set a stop-loss at $3 to cap your loss at $2 per contract.

2. Profit Targets

- Decide on a price level at which you'll exit the trade to secure profits.

- Example: If you aim for a 50% gain, sell the option when it reaches $7.50.

3. Trailing Stops

- Adjust your stop-loss as the trade moves in your favor to protect gains while allowing for further upside potential.

Position Sizing

Effective position sizing ensures you don't overcommit your capital to any single trade, reducing the impact of potential losses.

1. The 2% Rule

- Limit your risk on any single trade to 2% of your total trading capital.

- Example: If you have $10,000 in your account, your

maximum risk per trade is $200.

2. Consider Volatility

- Adjust position size based on the volatility of the underlying asset. Higher volatility may require smaller position sizes to manage risk.

3. Use Fractional Contracts

- Some brokers allow trading in fractional contracts, enabling you to fine-tune position sizes to align with your risk tolerance.

Avoiding Overexposure

Overexposure occurs when too much capital is allocated to a single trade, asset, or strategy, increasing overall portfolio risk.

1. Diversify Across Strategies

- Use a mix of strategies such as buying calls, selling

covered calls, and using spreads to balance risk and reward.

2. Avoid Concentration in One Asset

- Spread your trades across different underlying assets, sectors, or industries to reduce reliance on one market's performance.

Diversification in Options Trading

Diversification is a key principle in risk management, helping traders minimize the impact of losses from individual trades.

1. Strategy Diversification

- Combine speculative trades with hedging strategies to balance risk.

- Example: Use protective puts to offset potential losses in long stock positions.

2. Time Diversification

- Spread out your trades over different expiration dates to reduce the risk of timing the market incorrectly.

3. Asset Class Diversification

- Trade options on different asset classes, such as equities, indices, or commodities, to reduce exposure to a single market.

The Psychology of Risk

Successful options trading requires not only technical knowledge but also the ability to manage emotions and maintain discipline.

1. Managing Emotions in Trading

- **Fear:** Fear of loss can prevent traders from taking calculated risks or exiting losing trades on time.

- **Greed:** Greed can lead to overtrading or holding positions too long, resulting in missed profit opportunities or increased losses.

- **FOMO (Fear of Missing Out):** Avoid chasing trades based on others' successes or market hype.

2. Staying Disciplined

- **Stick to Your Plan:** Create a trading plan with defined rules for entry, exit, and risk management, and adhere to it consistently.

- **Avoid Revenge Trading:** Don't attempt to recover losses by taking impulsive, high-risk trades.

- **Maintain a Trading Journal:** Record your trades, strategies, and outcomes to identify patterns and areas for improvement.

Practical Tips for Risk Management

1. **Limit Leverage**

- Leverage amplifies both gains and losses. Use it cautiously and only when you fully understand the risks involved.

2. **Reassess Your Risk Tolerance Regularly**

- Risk tolerance can change over time due to factors like portfolio size, market conditions, or personal circumstances. Adjust your strategies accordingly.

3. **Monitor Trades Actively**

- Keep a close eye on your open positions to react swiftly to market changes.

4. **Use Risk Management Tools**

- Take advantage of tools like stop-loss orders, alerts, and analytics provided by your brokerage platform.

Notes:

- Effective risk management is essential to long-term success in options trading.

- Use tools like stop-loss orders, position sizing, and diversification to protect your capital.

- Recognize the psychological aspects of trading and strive to remain disciplined, even during periods of market volatility.

- By managing risks effectively, you can trade with

confidence and reduce the likelihood of catastrophic losses.

Chapter 7: Advanced Concepts (Optional for Ambitious Beginners)

Once you've grasped the basics of options trading and implemented beginner-friendly strategies, you may wish to explore advanced concepts to take your trading to the next level. This chapter introduces multi-leg strategies, explains how leverage can amplify both gains and losses, and highlights the impact of news and economic events on options prices. While these topics are optional, understanding them can offer significant advantages in navigating the complexities of the options market.

Multi-Leg Strategies

Multi-leg strategies involve combining two or more options contracts to create a position. These strategies allow traders to manage risk, increase profit potential, or benefit from specific market scenarios.

1. Spreads

Spreads involve simultaneously buying and selling options of the same type (calls or puts) but with different strike prices or expiration dates.

- **Bull Call Spread:**

- A bullish strategy that involves buying a call option at a lower strike price and selling another call option at a higher strike price.

- Example: If stock XYZ is trading at $50, you might buy a $45 call and sell a $55 call.

- **Benefit:** Reduces the upfront cost compared to buying a call outright.

- **Risk:** Limited to the net premium paid.

- **Bear Put Spread:**

- A bearish strategy that involves buying a put option at a higher strike price and selling another put option at a lower strike price.

- Example: If stock XYZ is trading at $50, you might buy a $55 put and sell a $45 put.

- **Benefit:** Limits losses while allowing participation in downside movements.

- **Risk:** Limited to the net premium paid.

2. Straddles and Strangles

These strategies are used to profit from significant price movements in either direction, often during periods of high volatility.

- **Straddle:**

- Involves buying a call and a put with the same strike price and expiration date.

- Example: Buying both a $50 call and a $50 put.

- **Benefit:** Profits from large price swings in either direction.

- **Risk:** Losses occur if the price remains stable, equal to the total premium paid.

- **Strangle:**

- Involves buying a call and a put with the same expiration date but different strike prices.

- Example: Buying a $45 put and a $55 call.

- **Benefit:** Costs less than a straddle but requires a larger price movement to be profitable.

- **Risk:** Similar to a straddle, but with slightly reduced premiums.

Understanding Leverage

Options inherently offer leverage, allowing traders to control a larger position with less capital than would be required for trading the underlying asset.

1. Benefits of Leveraging

- **Increased Profit Potential:** Amplifies returns on successful trades.

- **Capital Efficiency:** Allows traders to allocate less capital to achieve similar market exposure.

2. Dangers of Leveraging

- **Magnified Losses:** While profits can be amplified, so can losses.

- **Higher Risk of Overleveraging:** Taking on too many leveraged positions can deplete your capital quickly.

- **Time Decay:** Leveraged positions are particularly vulnerable to time decay (theta), which can erode their value over time.

The Impact of News and Events

Market-moving events can have a significant impact on options pricing and volatility. Advanced traders use these events to inform their strategies.

1. Earnings Announcements

- **Volatility Crush:** Implied volatility often rises leading up to an earnings announcement and drops sharply after, regardless of the result.

- **Trading Strategy:** Consider straddles or strangles to profit from anticipated volatility but exit positions before the announcement to avoid the crush.

2. Economic Indicators

- **Examples:** GDP reports, unemployment data, and

Federal Reserve announcements can affect broad market sentiment.

- **Impact on Options:** These events often increase implied volatility, creating opportunities for traders who anticipate the direction of the market.

Practical Examples of Advanced Strategies

Example 1: Bull Call Spread

- Stock XYZ is trading at $100.
- Buy a call option with a strike price of $95 for $7.
- Sell a call option with a strike price of $105 for $3.
- **Net Premium Paid**: $7 - $3 = $4.
- **Max Profit:** $10 (spread between strike prices) - $4 = $6 per contract.

Example 2: Earnings Straddle

- Stock ABC is trading at $50, with an earnings announcement due.

- Buy a $50 call for $3 and a $50 put for $2.
- **Total Premium Paid:** $5.
- If the stock rises to $60 or drops to $40, the profit is $5 ($10 movement - $5 premium).

Notes:

- Multi-leg strategies like spreads, straddles, and strangles allow traders to tailor risk and reward for specific market scenarios.
- Leverage can amplify profits but also increases risk, requiring careful management.
- News and events, such as earnings announcements and economic indicators, can create opportunities but demand precise timing and analysis.
- Ambitious beginners can explore these strategies with caution, starting small and thoroughly understanding the mechanics before scaling up.

Chapter 8: Tools and Resources for Options Traders

Mastering options trading requires the right tools, resources, and continuous learning. This chapter will guide you through essential trading tools, learning opportunities, and ways to practice without risking real money. By leveraging these resources, you can make informed decisions, stay updated on market trends, and refine your trading skills.

Essential Tools for Trading

Having the right tools at your disposal can streamline your trading process and enhance decision-making.

1. Charting Software

- Charting software helps visualize price trends, volatility, and trading volumes.
- Look for platforms that provide:
- Real-time data.

- Technical indicators like moving averages and Bollinger Bands.

- Historical data for analysis.

- **Popular Tools:** TradingView, Thinkorswim, and MetaTrader.

2. Economic Calendars

- Economic calendars provide schedules of key events, such as:

  - Earnings announcements.

  - Federal Reserve meetings.

  - Release dates for GDP, inflation, and employment reports.

- These tools help traders anticipate market volatility and plan strategies.

- **Popular Resources:** Investing.com, Forex Factory, and Bloomberg's Economic Calendar.

Learning from the Experts

Gaining insights from seasoned traders can accelerate your learning curve and provide valuable perspectives.

1. Recommended Books and Courses

- **Books:**

- *"Options as a Strategic Investment"* by Lawrence G. McMillan – A comprehensive guide to options strategies.

- *"The Options Playbook"* by Brian Overby – Beginner-friendly strategies with practical examples.

- *"Trading Options for Dummies"* by Joe Duarte – A simplified introduction to options trading.

- **Courses:**

- Online platforms like Udemy, Coursera, and Investopedia Academy offer beginner to advanced options trading courses.

- **Focus Areas:**

- Basics of options trading.

- Technical analysis.

- Risk management.

2. Webinars and Podcasts

- Many brokers and financial educators host live webinars on options trading strategies and market trends.

- Podcasts like Chat with Traders and Options Insider Radio provide insights from industry professionals.

Joining Online Trading Communities

Engaging with a community of traders allows you to exchange ideas, learn from others, and stay motivated.

1. Benefits of Online Communities

- Share trading experiences and strategies.

- Get real-time updates on market trends.

- Access valuable resources shared by experienced members.

2. Popular Communities

- **Reddit:** Subreddits like r/options and r/stocks.

- **Discord Groups:** Many trading-focused servers provide educational content and discussions.

- **Trading Forums:** Elite Trader and BabyPips forums offer interactive spaces for traders.

Practicing Without Risk

One of the best ways to develop your skills as a beginner is by practicing in a risk-free environment.

1. Using Demo Accounts

- Demo accounts simulate real trading environments without using real money.

- Benefits:

- Test strategies and understand the mechanics of trading platforms.

- Gain confidence before trading live.

- Experiment with advanced strategies, such as spreads or straddles.

    - **Platforms Offering Demo Accounts:**

    - Thinkorswim by TD Ameritrade.

    - Interactive Brokers.

    - eToro.

2. Paper Trading

- Paper trading involves manually tracking trades on paper or spreadsheets, allowing you to simulate trades without a platform.

- Advantage: Sharpens analytical skills without relying on platform automation.

Practical Steps to Get Started

1. **Choose Your Tools**

- Select charting software and an economic calendar that suit your needs.

2. **Build a Learning Plan**

- Read one recommended book per month or enroll in a course.

- Dedicate time weekly to listen to podcasts or attend webinars.

3. **Join a Community**

- Register for forums or join a Discord group to engage with experienced traders.

4. **Start Practicing**

- Open a demo account and practice placing trades.

- Use paper trading to backtest strategies against historical data.

Chapter 9: Building Your Options Trading Plan

Creating a well-structured trading plan is essential for success in options trading. A trading plan provides direction, keeps emotions in check, and helps you achieve consistent results. This chapter will guide you through setting clear goals, managing your risk, developing routines, and tracking your performance for continual improvement.

Setting Clear Goals

Your trading goals should align with your financial aspirations, risk tolerance, and time commitment.

1. Short-Term vs. Long-Term Objectives

- **Short-Term Goals:**
- Focus on immediate outcomes like learning specific strategies, making small profits, or reducing losses.
- Example: "Earn a 5% return on my initial capital in

the next three months."

- **Long-Term Goals:**

- Aim for sustainable growth and mastery of trading skills over time.

- Example: "Achieve a 20% annual return by following a disciplined trading routine."

2. SMART Goals

- Ensure your goals are Specific, Measurable, Achievable, Relevant, and Time-bound.

- Example: "Trade two contracts weekly, focus on covered calls, and limit losses to $100 per trade over six months."

Risk Tolerance and Capital Allocation

Understanding your risk tolerance and managing capital effectively are critical to avoiding significant losses.

1. Assessing Risk Tolerance

- Evaluate how much loss you can handle financially and emotionally.

- Categorize yourself as:

- Conservative: Prefer low-risk strategies like covered calls.

- Moderate: Willing to take calculated risks with strategies like buying calls or puts.

- Aggressive: Comfortable with high-risk strategies like spreads or leveraging.

2. Allocating Capital

- Follow the **2% Rule**: Never risk more than 2% of your total trading capital on a single trade.

- Example: With $10,000 in trading capital, risk only $200 per trade.

- Reserve a portion of your portfolio for safer investments to diversify your risk.

Developing a Trading Routine

Consistency is key to successful trading. Establishing a routine ensures you remain disciplined and prepared.

1. Market Analysis

- Dedicate time daily or weekly to analyze market trends, economic events, and volatility indicators.

- Use tools like charting software, news platforms, and economic calendars.

2. Trade Execution and Review

- Follow these steps:

- **Pre-Market Preparation:** Identify potential trades based on your strategy.

- **Trade Execution:** Place trades based on your analysis and set stop-loss/profit targets.

- **Post-Trade Review:** Evaluate the outcome and identify areas for improvement.

Tracking Your Progress

Monitoring your performance helps you identify strengths and weaknesses in your trading strategy.

1. Keeping a Trading Journal

- Record every trade in detail, including:
- Entry and exit points.
- Strategy used (e.g., buying calls, covered calls).
- Market conditions and analysis.
- Outcome (profit/loss).
- Example Entry:
- "Date: Jan 15, 2024. Strategy: Bull Call Spread on XYZ. Entry: Bought $50 call, sold $60 call. Outcome: 20% profit. Lesson: Entered during low implied volatility for optimal pricing."

2. Analyzing Wins and Losses

- Categorize trades into profitable and unprofitable.

- Look for patterns in losses:
- Were they caused by emotional decisions?
- Did you misjudge market trends?
- Adjust your strategies based on these insights.

Practical Steps to Build Your Trading Plan

1. **Define Your Objectives:** Write down short-term and long-term goals that align with your financial targets.

2. **Understand Your Risk:** Identify your risk tolerance and determine how much capital you can afford to allocate to trading.

3. **Create a Daily Routine:** Schedule time for market analysis, trade execution, and review.

4. **Document Everything:** Use a trading journal to track progress and refine strategies based on past performance.

5. **Regularly Review Your Plan:** Adjust your goals, risk tolerance, and strategies based on your evolving skills and market conditions.

Notes:

- Setting clear and achievable goals provides focus and motivation.

- Understanding your risk tolerance and using effective capital allocation prevents significant losses.

- A consistent trading routine ensures disciplined decision-making.

- Tracking and analyzing your progress through a trading journal is essential for continuous improvement.

Chapter 10: The Path Forward: From Beginner to Pro

As you wrap up your introduction to options trading, the journey is far from over. Moving from a beginner to a professional trader requires dedication, continuous learning, and a willingness to adapt. This chapter provides a roadmap for advancing your trading skills, staying informed about market trends, and embracing the growth mindset necessary for success.

Transitioning to Advanced Trading

Once you've mastered the basics, it's time to explore more sophisticated trading strategies and tools.

1. Expanding Knowledge of Strategies

- Delve deeper into multi-leg strategies:

- Spreads: Learn to use bull and bear spreads for directional plays.

- Iron Condors and Butterflies: Manage risk while maximizing potential profits.

- Understand the nuances of:

- Rolling Options: Adjusting positions to extend expiry dates or shift strike prices.

- Hedging Portfolios: Using options to mitigate risks in stock portfolios.

2. Exploring Futures and Other Derivatives

- Futures contracts can complement options trading by offering additional ways to hedge or speculate.

- Learn about other derivatives like swaps and forwards to expand your market knowledge.

- Assess the role of volatility products like VIX options and ETFs for advanced trading strategies.

The Importance of Continuous Learning

The financial markets are dynamic, and staying informed is essential for long-term success.

1. Staying Updated on Market Trends

- Follow economic news and updates on macroeconomic indicators such as interest rates, GDP, and inflation.

- Pay attention to sector-specific trends, like technology, energy, or healthcare, that could impact underlying assets.

2. Adapting to New Tools and Technologies

- Explore advancements in algorithmic trading and AI-powered analysis tools.

- Leverage platforms offering real-time analytics, customizable dashboards, and backtesting features.

- Stay updated with brokers offering cutting-edge resources for options traders.

3. Joining Professional Networks

- Participate in conferences, webinars, and seminars hosted by industry leaders.

- Engage with advanced online trading communities for insights on strategies and market developments.

Practical Steps for Progress

1. **Set New Goals**

- Transition from beginner strategies to intermediate and advanced techniques.

- Aim to master a specific set of strategies and track your results over time.

2. **Invest in Education**

- Attend advanced courses or obtain certifications in financial markets.

- Regularly update your knowledge through reading, webinars, and market research.

3. **Stay Consistent**

- Commit to a trading routine that includes preparation, execution, and review.

- Dedicate time to self-improvement and refining your skills.

Conclusion

Options trading is a powerful tool that opens up a world of opportunities for financial growth, strategic investing, and wealth-building. However, it's not without its challenges. This book has provided you with the foundational knowledge needed to navigate this complex yet rewarding market.

Embracing the Journey

Options trading is not a sprint—it's a marathon. There will be highs and lows, wins and losses, and moments of doubt. But with each trade, you will gain experience and insight, moving closer to becoming a skilled and confident trader.

- **Patience and Persistence Pay Off:** Success in trading rarely happens overnight. Stay committed to your trading plan, track your progress, and learn from every outcome.

- **Adaptability is Key:** Markets are unpredictable. The ability to adapt your strategies to changing conditions will set you apart.

Final Word of Encouragement

You don't need to be a financial genius to succeed in options trading. What you do need is curiosity, discipline, and the willingness to learn. Remember, every expert trader was once a beginner, just like you.

So, take a deep breath, step into the market with confidence, and remember: the power of derivatives is in your hands. Your journey is just beginning, and the possibilities are endless.

Here's to your success in the exciting world of options trading!

www.ingramcontent.com/pod-product-compliance
Lightning Source LLC
Chambersburg PA
CBHW070407230526
45471CB00006B/2692